ROOTS GREW WILD

ERICA HOFFMEISTER

PRAISE FOR ERICA HOFFMEISTER

*

In Roots Grew Wild, she [Erica] intertwines arresting and nurturing imagery from the natural world with the dramatic momentum of her coming-of-age narrative. Though you might need to break out the dictionary to look up some of the more obscure botany terminology, the emotional punch and passion of Hoffmeister's poetry stays with you. —*VIOLETA / GOODREADS REVIEWER*

*

This book was lovely—a rich and sensuous portrait of a landscape and a family that blossoms from the mundane and wild incidents of everyday life and into the very molecules of soil and animal and earth itself. —*SOPHIE / GOODREADS REVIEWER*

*

CONTENTS

I. RHIZOMA

Family Tree   1
Roots (pt. I)   2
The Middle   3
House   4
The Storm of '97   6
Moribund   7
Forest of Familiar Legs   8
Roots (pt. II)   9
In Memory   12
Over-Easy   13
My Mother's Secret   14
The Act   15
Camp Bald Cypress   16
Gas Station   18
South to Birmingham   19
Amazon   20
Dutch Twist   21
Roots (pt. III)   23
If You Sleep in a Treehouse   24

II. DENDROCHRONOLOGY

Arduous Vessels   29
Phylogenesis   30
Womb   31
Alveoli   32
How to Identify   33
Rhizoma   34
Things That Grow on Trees   35
The Collector   37
EcoSystem   38
Dendrochronology   39
A Thousand Plateaus   40

Roots Grew Wild is dedicated to my tallest sister, my muse.

I | RHIZOMA

FAMILY TREE

In time, you'll learn—this is what I was taught as a child, as a piece of furniture, switched on and off; a lamp at dusk. My glass held a universe of microorganisms, living creatures I could not see but knew were there. I drank them, and they made my body their home. It was I who wanted to be swallowed up. My feet were too heavy to swim and the river too cold to get lost in. To sink into the mud, into the world underneath the soppy layers, where even fish could not hide. I hid behind branches above the river.

Bark grew limbs that reached for one another across the banks. Where branches sprouted finger tips to touch and join forces, becoming one. Walked on planks, I wished for wings. The top too high, the air too thin, for I was but a girl. In the mornings I'd find another glass to drink from, another tree to climb.

ROOTS (PT. I)

Insects don't need trees like families need houses (or so my father told us) and for this, it was warranted.

Roots grew wild—reaching with, tiptoes and arm-length expanses to touch noses with other worlds, asking if trees grow upside down on the other side.

When I was a child our tree grew so large its roots broke through the house's foundation: a battle between bark and concrete, nature and ingredients, recipes we've fashioned to mimic the strength of the earth—on timeless soil we will always lay our swords down at the foot of any great tree.

Roots ran deep—under the earth, making pathways tunneling through time like wormholes into different dimensions.

My father took an axe—an element of the very thing it was made to destroy. He hit the tree once, twice, for several hours. Arms percolated with sweat, merging with bleeding sap of bark. From the porch, we could not tell who was a tree and who was a man, or whom the axe betrayed first.

THE MIDDLE

How could we know the world had already been dying?

Haunted between flickering neon, a buzz of lightning bugs, the humdrum glow in-and-out metronome in the chests of our breath—We caught eyes in pinpricked stars peeping through a dark void our parents named "sky."

The earth felt in disagreement with outer space—we belonged to the dirt.

In other words, it was the Fourth of July and Ruth ate one too many hot dogs—I hid behind tiny fireworks held in prepubescent hands sparkling on a stick, as all of summer seemed to sit.

My hands have looked the same since, the sky
no different.

HOUSE

1

Plastic forks and knives bent and twisted in shapes not meant for dishware; but then, this wasn't really our kitchen. It was once a wooden bench that housed a small bucket of rusted nails, hammers with splintered handles, a vice faded red around corners that we'd too often threatened to test the strength of each other's finger bones with. When we were tired of building birdhouses from cast-away tools we dusted particles of past projects from inside the grains of the oak wood bench and dragged it from the back shed to the spotted shade of the citrus trees which frosted over each winter, dying more and more with every passing season, with no end to our mother's persistence. It took the might of ten hands, ten feet, and several groans and bribes of ice cream cones. Trench trails uprooted weeds along the way as we made this into our new home. In that yellow apron, faded at the hips like a tent on a music box figurine: mother, we called her. Boys could never be one thing we decided, so they became all: brother, son, father, protector.

2

I, sanding each leg of our miniature kitchen, listened to chores define character, responsibilities outline fates. Titles we had been handed down without words or wrapped in holiday boxes, but through breastmilk and forehead kisses in church services and school bus stops. Assigned by the freckles on our cheeks and the number of dollars wadded up in the ankles of our socks where no one could find them. We were milkmaids, mechanics, housewives, and teachers. Mother, father, wife, son. Named not by birth order, but birth color, a chance roll of snake-eyed dice by a white-gloved doctor in a hospital uptown.

My mother wanted a water birth, as in, she wanted to wade as one with us in the river until we decided to swim outside her warmth. We were ripped from her womb as dry as dust—

3

Sawdust swirling in circles around September leaves. Piles of certainty: certainty that the leaves would crash into earth and course through veins underground by month until green sprouts welcomed spring in a rush of pollen and migraines, mothers always seemed to turn up with at the sight of a new sun. Her, in that yellow apron, faded at the hips, silly and small playing house: they called her mother. She raised her tiny hand to her temple and squinted her eyes hard. I had it easy, always playing myself.

THE STORM OF '97

It rained bullets in shotgun sprays, shards of metal
opening up the earth into tiny crevices; each moment
spattered in slow-motion.

We have to stay inside today, our father said.

But it was the first day of summer,
and we had just turned on the sprinkler.
Walls of lead-laced droplets collaborated in dance with
the falling sky, orbiting in the green air as one motion.

He smelled like rotten eggs, sulfur breathed into open
palms, fogging up the glass. Imprinted into our skinfolds
we watched time pass safely from the window for the next
three months.

MORIBUND

Her morning blouse always needed ironing,
the lemon dish soap scent on her wrists forgave this.

Occupied in aprons and feathers, we avoided embraces
that could not be answered.

In bubbles, we hid from the things
we were afraid of, interlocking fingers

when no one came sweeping in to check night-lights, to
investigate footprints in the carpet or creaks in weathered
floorboards.

For there were already monsters under our beds;
fogs of darkness hung in the corners of our bedroom
ceiling

as if the morning sunrise could eat the blackness for
breakfast—
then, our delicate hearts could mend and brighten

through the yellow haze in a bright blue sky,
like lemon and blueberries

and other things
that do not rhyme with bruises.

and the soft spot beneath his collarbone, a pool of skin riding waves as he moved his neck and caught me, my gaze on the dancing brown mole rising and falling with every breath.

I would find myself lost there for hours: with my father asleep on his favorite chair, or sometimes on the porch cleaning my brothers' pellet gun while spitting tobacco, the mole jumping more violently in surprise then.

Or sometimes, I'd wonder if my mother lost herself too, in the crook in his neck. If that's where she fell in love if that's where she went to hide on the days, we only saw her in passing shadows, down the hall her muffled cries.

No need for asking, for saying things like *I love you*—there were smiles deep in denim pockets and a firm palm scratchy to the touch on peach cheeks. There was a comfort in the silence of the sunrise, him thinking through black coffee and rubbing firefly guts all over our bicycles without telling us until mid-summer.

He was in the forest as we ran through it, the same timber used to build our front porch, our bunk beds, what kept us warm through winter. Warm, I was—muzzled tight in the soft crook of his neck.

ROOTS (PT. II)

Their noses were pushed up against the glass like three little pigs, streaks of bubbling drool sliding across the front window in cinematic drama. My three brothers watched wide-eyed as our father removed his flannel shirt button by button and scanned the tree up, down, up, down, several minutes passing in anticipation while the syncopated beat of tobacco chew snapping and spitting kept my heart's meter pounding through each wrinkle of bark. His eyes followed up to the tip-top of my favorite branch where I perched in a gargoyle stance. My eyes found my sister one level below me, her hands wound tightly around her mouth, holding in her silence.

His shirt fell to his feet.

He gripped the axe and each finger fell across the wooden handle as if playing the piano. It was an old axe, reddened with rust and splintering at the bottom, famous for digging holes in the palms of those unlucky enough to be punished with splitting wood. Not his hands, no—his skin calloused and thick as tree bark, he raised the axe over his head, let it rest on his shoulder for a moment, wrinkled his nose at the boys in the window, and swung. I felt the impact ripple and roar, growing in power as it resounded through each layer of tertiary branches that no longer seemed as sturdy a fortress as we first trusted.

We trembled in a sudden sharp fear which reddened our faces and whitened our grips. Thunderclap followed thunderclap, the axe finding a home in the deeper and deeper crevice each time. My sister bellowed beneath her breath—my father unstoppable.

I was a warrior. In a blood oath alliance to my tree given in every scrape, every splinter. Every summer's day spent through bites of dripping sweet peaches under the shade of its thick leaves; every board ripped from the dilapidated shed out back and nailed to its trunk by my hand; every bird's nest prudently placed and protected by my heart. Because it was I who raked fallen leaves each Autumn; I who was the only to reach the tip-top branch and find the North Star peep-holed through the clearest of Midwestern night skies; I who taught my brothers how to climb barefoot onto newly green leaves and tender May branches. Surrender or sacrifice, my soul had been spoken for.

Bark began to bleed, palms stuck in sap and glued into an immovable grip. One final blow rested in the bark's crevice, a tremor unsticking her tiny hands.

She tumbled midair in a cloud of slow movement, scratching at the sky, pulling leaves to her chest in desperate tufts. But I was still stuck, and she now a puff of dirt. Wails freed from the pits of her body. At once, crumpled at the roots of the tree, bone erupting from her forearm like a stick in the mud, her face blanched pale as milk, blood red as my father's eyes. The drop seemed a swift mile when she fell, but for me, a moment.

My wrist twisted in my father's sun-hardened hand, pulling my bones apart as he dragged me diagonally, the balls of my feet digging trenches behind us across the dirt driveway. Tossed hard into the back of our blue Buick, a heavy door slammed against my body as a cinder block prison cell wall, my throat choking on defeat in thick gurgles. He walked back to the base of the tree and scooped up her limp body, draping her softly across his broad shoulders. She was a casualty of war. And in her alliance, it was I who would be held responsible. The three little piglets burst out of the front door, and as boys so typically do, poked and prodded her flesh with twigs in circles around their path to the car. Ruth lay gently in the front seat on my mother's lap, the three boys and I urgently squeezed in the back. Over rocks and potholes, we drove away. My body motionless as I watched my father slog the axe head back to the tree.

As we turned the corner onto the road, all I could see was a blur of movement as he swung again.

IN MEMORY

That was my past life.

Strong, like an Amazon

My father beats his chest and the boys follow,
but I know it's meant for me.

meant white membrane turned to rubber, cased the yolk tight and shiny as a lightbulb sparked at the switch. To run slow as sunny molasses—a gentle pop by a silver fork at the exact right moment.

That's how he liked to do it—over-peppered—and it drove my mother crazy. Over-hard, cooked like slippery rocks from the river, she might as well have hard-boiled hers. The runny yolks were too wild—they slipped down her throat; embryos making their way through life backward, and while we didn't even have a rooster, she'd sometimes stare at the chicken feet poking holes through the sizzle in the frying pan as she cooked them.

I'd ask for mine sunny side up. Not because of the name that made my sister giggle each time (*would sunny side down mean dinner eggs?*), or because it made me think of 6 am morning chores the days after I'd stayed out too late, foliage wrapped up in braids and dirt smeared in the crevices behind my knees. It was the bubbling of the yolk freely dancing in bacon grease for too long, it was the way she salted them with sadness.

MY MOTHER'S SECRET

It was in the way she said *okay*, by simply nodding. Though if you looked close enough at the fine lines around her mouth, her lips twitched a tell so deep, the bucket's rope could never reach her.

THE ACT

It took nine hours to chop down the tree.

Once it had fallen, he tied cables to the thicker branches and used the tractor to haul it to the back of the house. It sat in three pieces next to the woodpile. He took a shovel and dug deep around the remaining stump, between the immense root system that shot in every direction in the dirt. With a pickaxe, he broke through fibers that had fed the tree for decades. He used his own weight for leverage to snap and tear its ligaments with a crowbar, then pulled the stump from the ground in grunting heaves and long exhales. Borrowed breaths of recycled oxygen.

I wondered if he noticed how much it had bled, how the ants retreated into the soil searching for a new home. He had developed new blisters in his hands; muscles ached in victory.

The old splintered axe leaned against the trunk invitingly.

was offshore, about a mile south. From our platform hidden in the treetops, we could see the rhythmic splash of bodies splitting the water in two from a high rope swing over the bulbous roots of the bald cypress trees that had claimed the muddy banks as their permanent foothold. Our own feet dangled like fishing lures over the river, though we were the ones being taunted and teased from afar. We weren't the city kids whose Los Angeles parents in Ray-Bans and flip-flops packed perfect paisley suitcases with SPF 40 sunblock (we used mud, the aloe Vera planted outside the kitchen window) or "first aid kits" (our knee-scrapes had whisky breath). In the afternoons, you could hear a faint whistle from a red-bodied lifeguard who taught them how to swim—we were thrown in and learned how not to drown.

One summer, when I was the only woman in my family not particular to dresses, I found myself bushwhacking too close to their pristine trails marked with tie-offs red like blood against earth's camouflage. I, the shape of rustling branches, was caught dead in silent footfalls by marooned laughter a few short steps from my own bare feet. There were two of them—other. Girls sun-tanned with stick-straight hair from tip to follicle, as shiny as sour lemonade. One carrying an oversized towel, the other a cassette player, they trotted heavy-footed in an exotic wilderness to feel bug bites under tiny breasts and clay between virgin toes as they gasped and giggled at the soft white under-skin of older camp counselors. Cherry lips hidden under manicured hands; all for only a week or two to have something to write home about. For a moment I swayed forward; perhaps I, too, was from New York City, or maybe just the only child of a suburban home tucked safely in another Midwestern town slightly west. It must have been my feet that gave me away—at the sight of theirs, I ran.

GAS STATION

She was eleven, but the way he was staring at her mouth he could've guessed at least sixteen.

I was sixteen, but the way my narrow shoulders met her chest made her look ever taller, broader, like a map laid across a table and pressed from corner to corner, asking your fingertips to run across water ridge lines with your smooth spinning compass pointing south.

I took the cherry sucker from her mouth and popped it in my own.
Hey! She screeched, with the tone of a girl who had just gotten her period for the first time, her knees still unaccustomed to the weight of dying blood.

He lost us in gas-stained coveralls, looked back to the pump, sweat on the wrists.

The sucker protruded my cheek like an abscess, rotting my back teeth
until I threw it at our feet.

SOUTH TO BIRMINGHAM

On the back of a train, she discovered the beauty in goodbye, how the tallest trees said their last.

Each drop of rain that fell from the sky that day was off the tips of her fingers—the only person I knew to wave with her wrist at her hips.

Seventeen, the train tracks rumbled beneath her footsteps.
Seventeen, the August air billowed in battered breaths when she bit her bottom lip on toes rocking back and forth from heel to ball to heel to ball, a hand on the tiniest plaid-handled box we'd ever seen.

With her hair unbraided, trestles whipped at her waistline exposed to green mist and trees none of us had the chance to name yet.

The train's whistle made my bird-boned mother jump from her ankles, but I was always there to press her shoulders back down into her breasts. I caught my little sister's right eye over her shoulder blade, that twitch-one-two-three-four of her eyelashes as she boarded:

I'll miss you, too

AMAZON

My eyes find my sister's pregnant belly, pursed full under denim overalls, pushing, pushing out towards the world, limbs stretched and pulsing under pale flesh she won't let us see or touch ourselves. I suppose it's her way of keeping the baby her own. Evading invasion—unsolicited prodding and poking, cheeks to her ribs listening, wondering, making expert suggestions and jealous coos at a life not yet here, but so immediately here, and with every passing moment becoming more and more itself and less and less her.

She's only nineteen but we feel as if time has been burned in the stove's belly. Her always silent demeanor now an effigy of strength. Balance. Sloppy waddles are replaced with confident strides. An Amazon woman stomping tree-trunk legs onto the earth demanding:

we are here to stay

DUTCH TWIST

Arms and legs braided—
a closeness
that can only be so tightly wound
with the skin of sisters. She counts:
one, two, three, four

The syncopation of beating hearts in
the darkness, beaded sweat bleeding
from forehead to forehead:
one, two, three, four

Mother tied ribbons around our necks
the color of your eyes, the color of
blood before
it curdles in the open air. Oxidation—
veins blue, green, the yellow
-ing of skin before the storm.
See, that's just not true—blood
is red. It runs through bodies of trees and
scales of fish and gets caught in our fingertips, throbs
as life often does:
one, two, three, four

Maple syrup courses over valley
floors and through streams and waterways
to feed our forest life, to
decorate pancakes made with sawdust. When
our family dog died, she left a hole
in the carpet where I used to lay— maroon darkened
from oils that had leaked through skin and follicle, as if
she never left. Replaced by a seed planted
deep in Ruth's belly, I wanted to run
where the syrup could not stretch. To a garden
sewn by time and circumstance, by who, we were never
told.

If I were seven again, I could hold my sister's hand deep
in the forest where we buried
our childhood, where we twisted together
the long locks of our hair in the afternoon shade.

She tells me to count with her:
one, two, three, four

ROOTS (PT. III)

Limbs crawled backward in time, exposing crumbles of
living flesh from under our house.

If I crawl into the space where the tree used to be, I can
hear it breathing—
a ghost of lingering dust so small we can only taste it if
the breeze is still.

We sat in gaps of time, waiting for it to return with our
tongues reaching toward one another's to China, to
Antarctica, to space. To the stars,
where planets grow their own trees, versions of axes held
upside down,
houses too soft to rebuild when the roots keep growing.

Bulbous and grand it once was, now
space.

Time hacked down through each ring. Ageless in death
and
born into another purpose,
or so we believed on Sundays. A forest
full of them, anyway, he had said.

For our trees, we lied to ourselves—uprooted
from a foundation made of crumbles.

IF YOU SLEEP IN A TREEHOUSE

1

You are that much closer to the stars, my mother told us in crouched whispers. It was just my sister and me then, our lives still quiet as two in twin braids and the habit of speaking to each other in Morse code by squinting our eyes. It was because of this I never learned how to properly wink and would spend an evening at my first high school dance in a corner after being convinced that it was the kind of thing boys liked (but only if you did it right, I learned). This was long before treehouses signified stolen kisses under a full moon—still figuring how to breathe out of your nose, tongue spilling around raspberry-tart lips.

Before our brothers popped out one by one from underneath our mother's skirt and claim-jumped our dry-rotten shamble fort with a shared pellet gun, us mere girls labeled trespassers. It was before the forest fire opened up a gap in the tree line, providing a view from the back window we never wanted: an apocalypse scene in a charred black half-moon shape, better left by a falling asteroid.

2

We never wanted to see across the river from our bedrooms—we were still young enough to be afraid of the forest. Deep mud at night harvesting toad's eyes sunk into quicksand, armies of crooked men luring over virgin pathways lit by planets, before we knew the moonlight was a reflection. With no tree of our own, we had begged our father to build us a castle in the treetops, wrapped tall around bark as camouflage, opened with a heavy iron key into a secret passage, revealing a platform so high in the clouds that our parents looked like insects—the same insects we'd capture and pull apart and put back together in pieces.

3

Our imagination served us disappointment in the form of two-by-fours and rusty nails, a half-day's job by a man who didn't believe *in* building in trees because trees were made to be built *with*. And now, we had to sleep in our treehouse by the river. As the sun set in moments our fingers grasped each other's in tighter pulses; by now my mother thought we inherited a tick, perhaps we needed glasses, or a therapist, or perhaps, a safe bed. With a knapsack slung off my shoulder we journeyed into the underbrush, our imaginations trading in the word *disappointment* for *unrestrained* as we were led by wild shadows and flame-orange bursts of light peeking through trees that suddenly looked foreign. It was an adventure, I told her, reminding her of what my mother said about stars although we both thought the stretched black canvas over sky pockmarked with dead light was terrifying. A feeling close enough to touch but always a cardboard-arm length too far to reach.

Trailblazers, we were; wondering if we should have left a trail of bread behind us, beckoning The Ozark Howler. I wished for summer, for lightning bugs, for the ease of warm water lapping against the low river banks under a buzz of cicadas. It was cold; a lesson, perhaps. We fell asleep with pressed foreheads, the knapsack unopened and used instead as a blanket for our elbows in the still silence of a cool, moonless night, and never returned again.

II | DENDROCHRONOLOGY

ARDUOUS VESSELS

Thus, began a long period of acceptance: bone marrow nourishes blood vessels, tortured anatomy, rehabilitation. How fingernails keep growing after death. Bird's beaks do the same thing. Can you hear them? Flowing in both directions—I know this is impossible, but it happens. Often, a dilation will occur when the insomniac beast wins the battle, thundering hooves at night rippling under open windows. In waves, the wind hits each branch one by one, the hemlines last; lace is too fragile to blow away at the kneecaps. A chill inside the joints, fresh and wounded. I shot a deer when I was five, and never forgot the sound of it. Can you tell me which way to row? The paddles were drowned last winter, the only year it froze completely over, the year we lost our horse to the flesh-eaters. Amend it, mislabeled, like my eye-color and how no one quite knows how to pronounce the word *mountain*.

PHYLOGENESIS

The evolution
of everything that came after
you

The evolution
of everything that came

The evolution
of
you

WOMB

Say it aloud: *womb*

Notice how your lips meet at the corners, a soft hum rises from the back of your mouth, the vowel shapes itself the color of flesh taking pieces of you with it as it curves over your tongue in admiration for the letter "o" and the power in changing sound, in making something from nothing, nothing from something, and when the letters pushed together to create this word now fashioned to your body like a badge on the lapel, it closes the tip of your upper lip over the slight gap you inherited from your mother that you never liked and presses just so, meeting wetness at the bottom in a reverbed release of the word.

It isn't only yours anymore—you gave it up in shared parcels the moment you said it.

ALVEOLI

In breathing spaces hidden, there are much larger lungs
to find
three-hundred million balloons in a hollow cavity.

With room for empty spaces, we've connected ourselves
with tissue.
Flesh bonds together with the spit of our ancestors, wall
unbreakable

as bone and muscles and skin before each is ripped into
tiny chards
breathed in as ash in the lungs like charred tree branches
in a locked box.

My favorite has always been the respiratory tree,
branches thin spawn offshoots
I've searched under, over ground for a latex sac caught
low in the rhizomes.

HOW TO IDENTIFY

elderberries from their poisonous doppelgangers, find
wild garlic and dig ginseng, what leaves to press on open
wounds, and which would only cause their own—

There are no home-remedies in the forest—there are no

                                            forest-

                        remedies in the

                home.

RHIZOMA

Detached from the beginning—
seed, watered
stretched skin in soft soil
mended, coddled, shined
in spring sun
rays warm— spun metal
a mass

Of people, of memory. Together,
it has formed who you are. Apart, you
are nothing. This is your family—broken

limbs that grow from saplings, a ripped
root into a tree, nevertheless. Haunted
waters filling space, sacs of
blood and bones identical from under
a microscope—cradling circumstance as the infinite
erasure of self.

To find myself tangled from within, unknowing whose
skin
I belong to.

THINGS THAT GROW ON TREES

If you've ever dissected soil, you've found the beating
heart of earth. It's always bothered me
how easily things bleed from one another (sap, molasses,
lemon juice stinging sore cuticles)
and effortlessly into something else (rivers, bloodstreams,
bee's wings, umbilical cords).

Nature praises transformation (evolution) the plump
caterpillar's feet exchanged for butterfly's wings for just a
few days of flight in spring. But what if I didn't want to be
that delicate, or that beautiful, or that
short-lived?

I was a stout-legged caterpillar, who dug her poisoning
horns into dirt and enjoyed it— who burrowed holes into
as many tomatoes and oranges and baby-green leaves as
she could.
I moved in waterfalls within me, in the camouflage palette
of safety, collecting things that grow on trees and
suspending them in dewdrop prisons.

The cocoon seemed to sew itself together without my
consent at the moment
of conception—

the trickling of blood down crescent thighs bow-legged
and solitary,
suddenly unable to run because
suddenly I had only
two.

In a force rotated inward, I didn't think to fight gravity—
I lost each ring around my belly and climbed in without
asking why.

Perhaps it was just time. A biological clock, as they said—
this was just nature and within three days' time, I learned

I couldn't hold myself up
with just two fragile wings.

THE COLLECTOR

I found little things: the shape of finger's webs, the taste of finger bones raw from gnawing on them in early mornings before the sun appeared like a drop of water on oil spots in the driveway. Swirled magic sky on fire in freezing air—

an empty box.

The collector of things: acorn families rested in elbows, leaf dust in pimento jars on windowsills, low autumnal light by mouthfuls kept behind back molars to last through winter.

Replace the joints with stones, pronounce vowels with awkward transitions, pinch skin between bootlaces and remember how painful it is to catch nettle under toenails. Hibernate the memories in a stop-motion robotic flow cold as a reptile's bones, strung over doorjambs the day's everything smelled like maceration. Heavy bone-lust and chalkboard dust coughed from lungs, black clouds on breakfast plates, pillowed death, an obsession emptied

out of pockets with the rest.

ECOSYSTEM

A beetle is but a beetle, or so one thinks of very small
things. Mud wet with earth
sodden, weighted, each layer heavier than the first. In
leaves, we counted veins and matched them with our
own. These were maps to the otherworld.

One cannot follow the treetop breeze—
it sounds like a rough ocean without a single shell.

Canopy, strong. Branches, thin. Roots, deep. Without
one,
there cannot be mud. Without mud, there is no earth.
There is no water, or so I am told.

Invasive species crawl in unannounced, and we find
holes
in the bushes where we left them. This is our evidence of
deconstruction. Of loss. Of a downtrodden passage
sunken
into wildlife long forgotten.

If you follow the footsteps downriver, you'll find a path
tunneling through trees—
components in a biological infrastructure: a foundation
of wooden people who can only grow up or down, but
never side to side without touching.

Hack it down, I thought. Let's start over. In a world
without trees.

DENDROCHRONOLOGY

We mark the molding with crayon,
her stomach with twine, the treehouse pail
with heavy stones.

We counted moments as minutes in
time-locked rotations neither one of
us asked to be responsible for knowing.

Human rivers flow, dead-stopped still
if the counting stops.

The beetles burrow deep into tree rings
drills to keep moving. When I stopped counting
lost dust between the years,
the inches, belt loops, ribbons fell in dirt
mounds. I counted

backward then, put the child back in,
discover intricate mazes lost with a whistle
of dirt blown harder, the wooden rings
uncountable, you—uncountable,

perished, petrified

my dendron mystic:
seventy-three rings to keep us alive.

A THOUSAND PLATEAUS

It is all illuminated when you're alone:

The way wind cuts
through grass
at the stem, at the soil—
The sound of loved ones' laughter
mangled together, the memory indistinguishable
from one's own night
sky separated from the night air
when up here, it's on fire
long after you're asleep.

The loud sound of the creek water
left behind—
a sunburn on your back right shoulder,
empty picture frame in a suitcase,
the distinct taste of a stolen afternoon
cigarette, of a kiss
521 miles away
from a woodpecker on a soft bank
debating the temperature of rippling water,
accepting his solitude, an image
of thought—
seeing the world
just as it is.

ERICA HOFFMEISTER IN CONVERSATION

WHAT INSPIRED ONE OF YOUR POEMS?

Some of my poems are from the heart, drawn from raw experience and emotion, while others are 100% fictionalized, and I'm writing from the perspective of an imagined narrator. Regardless, there is usually some sort of personal inspiration that triggers a poem, something in the well of my life that I'll draw from as a genesis point. A good example of something in between is the poem "The First." I wrote it as an emotional response to finding out about my younger sister's pregnancy. Though that really happened, and I really did feel the way the narrator does in the poem, I didn't write it as myself – I wrote it into the overarching narrative that became *Roots Grew Wild*, in a totally different world with different people, living totally different, yet similar experiences.

WHAT IS AN OBSCURE THING YOU FIND INTERESTING ABOUT THE WORLD?

So, someone—a planetary geologist—had their ashes sent to the moon after he died. So, there's technically a graveyard up there. Which is possibly the most unique after-death "burial" I've ever heard of. I think it's interesting how much we think about what happens to our bodies after death—what we do to them, how we dispose of them, respecting the dead with these certain cultural idiosyncrasies—is it for us, or for the people we leave behind after we die? I don't know if its obscure, but it has always interested me how different cultures have their own "normal" to cope with the human body left behind after death. It makes you wonder why we obsess about what we want to happen to our bodies at that point—if it's all self-reflective, projection, or fear of death itself. Essentially, I think it's superstition—but, so is basically everything when it comes to human rituals; the need for some sort of control, even after we're gone.

WHAT ODD, FUNNY OR INTERESTING FACT CAN YOU SHARE ABOUT YOUR WRITING HABITS OR PROCESS?

I am so boring, I feel like. I write for an hour or two every morning while my daughter is just waking up and doing her own morning routine. I'm a busy, working mom so that's all the time I get for writing, and I carve it out with a dull knife just to get that much – so I have to find other ways to "write," such as mulling over ideas and words while I go on runs or drive to work, jotting down ideas in my Notes app on my phone or scribbling things down on scraps of paper as I teach or bartend, or literally at any other given time. Sometimes nothing at all comes of any of these thoughts and notes – nothing material, anyway. But, I like to encourage the idea that a writer never stops writing. Alicia Mountain wrote this piece, "Concerning Craft: To the Writer Who is Not Writing," where she says:

"Writer, you are living a life, even if it is humble or meager in ways. Writing comes out of this life lived, the sensory details, the doubt, the microwaved dinner, the weight of your jacket, the joy, the car payment, the lonely shower, the movement of your body. Everything you do away from your notebook or keyboard is writing. Even if it fills months or years, you can make use of it—this can all end up on the page. You know this."

This hit me hard, because I internalize writer's guilt a lot—that feeling of lack of productivity, that without tangible proof on a daily basis, I do not deserve the title of "writer." But a writer's life is constantly building and writing; our writing "process" includes more than just the words we end up with, it is every moment before those words even hit the page.

HOW IMPORTANT IS LANGUAGE AND/OR WORD CHOICE TO YOUR WRITING?

I mean language is writing is language is word choice is writing, right? You can't really disconnect any of it – especially in poetry, when you can hang on writing one word for an entire day or more. It has to be the right word; there has to be no other possible word within known language, real or imagined, that is destined to fit in that exact place, in that specific line, in that particular poem. Sometimes the language emerges from the unknown place—that center of the writing mind, spills right out—and sometimes it takes hours reading, searching, digging for what is meant to be... Long answer long, yes! Without a deep obsession with language and words and how they create whole worlds out of simple shapes we call letters... well, I wouldn't be here.

ARE THERE ANY THEMES OR REOCCURRING THREADS THAT YOU TRY TO EXPLORE IN YOUR WRITING?

Generally, if I'm writing and something particularly thematic keeps popping up in different stories and poems, that's when I think: "OK, I've got a collection forming here," and then I might try to explore those things at a deeper, more intentional level – because obviously, my writing mind is considering it important at that time. From there, a sort of narrative or theme may blossom from the inside out – but we tend to work together as a team, the creator and created. I don't usually go into my writing time thinking: "Today, I'm going to write a poem about sisterhood," or whatever, not to say that never happens, either, though.

IS THERE SOMETHING YOU FIND PARTICULARLY DIFFICULT ABOUT THE WRITING PROCESS?

Every poem I write is, at its center, a story. That's what I find so beautiful about poetry – it is not so much about the poem itself, but the world that the poem exists in. This is where I'm entering when I write a poem, and it takes time to fully develop that world in order to complete a poem that is authentic and makes sense to me. I can't just spit out conceptual imagery or emotion – or if I am writing from my gut, stream of consciousness style, I still go back to what I wrote and figure out "ok, where did this come from? What reality do these concept exist in? What is the story here?" I am obsessed with the underlying narratives of everything and everyone around me – and poetry is that beautiful, momentary glimpse into things unrevealed or unsaid. This obsession is time consuming and at times, mentally exhausting —especially when writing a simple, short poem that may only actually be a few lines.

WHAT OTHER ART FORM [IF ANY] INFLUENCES OR INFORMS YOUR WRITING? E.G. FILM, MUSIC, PAINTING / VISUAL ART...

Everything. Is that understated enough? Ha. I mean, I've written a deep vat of love poems heavily influenced by me reading War and Peace at the time, and I've written about how it feels to listen to Led Zeppelin in the summertime with all the car windows down after listening to "Houses of the Holy" at a really watershed moment in my life, and I've written deeply about my love and gratitude for Buffy the Vampire Slayer. I am a conglomerate of influences, mentored by the poetry within literally every form of art.

WHAT IS YOUR MOST RECENT WORK AND WHERE CAN READERS FIND IT?

Of course, KITW—my first chapbook Roots Grew Wild is just published! I also have a cross-genre piece that is, in rare form, not fictionalized at all, but rather personal, recently published in Mom Egg Review's quarterly VOX, titled "Aversion." Also, my first full length hybrid collection, Lived in Bars is forthcoming from Stubborn Mule Press TBA in 2019, and some of the flash-prose that can be read in the meantime from that book include: "The Mission Inn," published in Fiction Southeast, and "Pops," and "The Bum Steer," published in Abstract Magazine in their online journals throughout this year as well. All my previously published work, and work to come, can be found on www.ericarhoffmeister.com.

ABOUT THE AUTHOR

Erica Hoffmeister holds an MFA in Creative Writing and has both poetry and fiction published in various journals and magazines. Born in Southern California but always living elsewhere, she spends her days teaching, writing, and perpetually missing home -- wherever that feels like at the time.

Find her on:

Instagram / Twitter: @zephyrstardust
Website: www.EricarHoffmeister.Com

COPYRIGHTS

KINGDOMS IN THE WILD PRESS

Is the place for original, experimental, and cutting-edge poetry and fiction. We strive to bring you work that reflects the world's complex and intertwined cultures and histories. Join the conversation by visiting our site today <u>KINGDOMSINTHEWILD. COM</u>

www.ingramcontent.com/pod-product-compliance
Lightning Source LLC
Chambersburg PA
CBHW021942040426
42448CB00008B/1189